PICTURE LIBRARY

POISONOUS INSECTS

POISONOUS INSECTS

Norman Barrett

Franklin Watts

New York   London   Toronto   Sydney

©1991 Franklin Watts

Franklin Watts, Inc.
387 Park Avenue South
New York NY 10016

Printed in the United Kingdom

Library of Congress Cataloging-in-Publication Data

Barrett, Norman S.
    Poisonous insects/Norman Barrett.
        p. cm. — (Picture library)
    Includes index.
    Summary: A look at the ways various insects use poison in self-
defense or to capture their prey.
    ISBN 0-531-14152-7
    1. Insects — Juvenile literature. 2. Arthropoda, Poisonous —
Juvenile literature. 3. Animal defenses — Juvenile literature.
[1. Insects. 2. Predatory animals. 3. Animal defenses.]
I. Title. II. Series.
QL467.2.B37 1991
595.7057—dc20   90-46256
                                                      CIP AC

Designed by
Barrett and Weintroub

Research by
Deborah Spring

Picture Research by
Ruth Sonntag

Photographs by
Heather Angel (pages 12, 25t)
S.C. Bisserot (page 10)
Michael Chinery (pages 6, 17, 22t, 23, 26)
Pat Morris (pages 11, 18b)
Natural Science Photos/C.F.E. Smedley
    (front cover)
Natural Science Photos (pages 7, 16, 18t,
    19, 25b, 27, 30)
Survival Anglia (pages 2, 3, 13, 14, 15,
    20–21, 22b, 24, 28, 29, back cover)

Illustration by
Rhoda and Robert Burns

Technical Consultant
Michael Chinery

Contents

Introduction

There are two main types of poisonous insects: those with weapons such as stings and those that have poison in their bodies.

Bees, wasps and some ants are stinging insects. Bees, and some wasps, use their stings in self-defense. Some ants and wasps use theirs to kill prey. Some beetles and flies inject harmful substances by biting. Insects with poison in their bodies include some bugs, beetles, moths and butterflies.

△ A wasp feeding. Most poisonous insects have bright markings. These act as a warning. Any animal that disturbs or attacks a wasp or a bee is likely to be stung.

Most of the insects that use poison for defense have special markings or are brightly colored. This warns animals that feed on insects to leave them alone. Insects with warning coloration include many bees, wasps, bugs, and moths.

Some caterpillars have hairs or bristles that cause irritation. They do this by injecting a poison.

Some flies are regarded as poisonous or harmful insects because they spread disease.

△ The caterpillar of a South American moth. Moths, butterflies and their caterpillars do not have stings. But many have poison in their bodies and some caterpillars have dangerous stinging hairs.

Looking at poisonous insects

Warning coloration

Some insects display colors that tell predators to keep away. Bright red and black, or yellow and black stripes or spots are a sign that the insect is dangerous to eat. Other creatures soon learn to recognize these signals and leave the insects alone.

Monarch butterfly

Cinnabar moth caterpillar

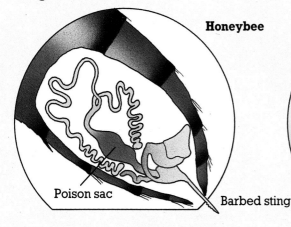

Stings

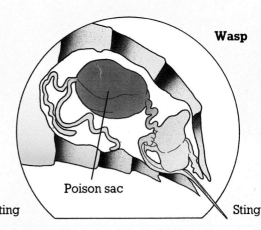

Honeybee

Poison sac

Barbed sting

Wasp

Poison sac

Sting

Bee stings have a barbed end which catches in the victim's body. The honeybee cannot pull its sting out without dislodging the whole sting structure from its own body. So using its sting means death for the unfortunate honeybee.

The stings of wasps and bumblebees are not extremely barbed, so they can easily withdraw them. Stinging causes no damage to the wasp, which lives to sting again.

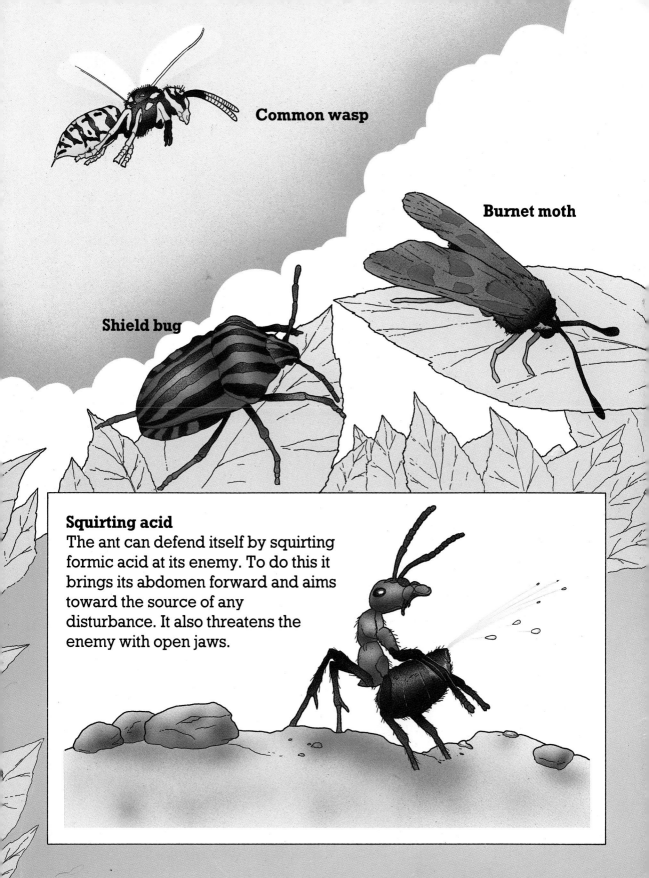

Common wasp

Burnet moth

Shield bug

Squirting acid
The ant can defend itself by squirting formic acid at its enemy. To do this it brings its abdomen forward and aims toward the source of any disturbance. It also threatens the enemy with open jaws.

Bees

Bees are found in all parts of the world except the polar regions. There are about 20,000 species (kinds) of bees. Most species are solitary bees – they live alone.

Some bees, such as bumblebees and honeybees, live and work together in colonies. They are called social bees. A colony consists of a queen, other female bees called workers, and male bees called drones. Only the females have stings – used to defend the colony.

△ A bumblebee lands on a flower to find the pollen and nectar that bees live on. They make honey from the nectar. As they move from flower to flower, they spread pollen, enabling the flowers to reproduce.

▷ A colony of honeybees. They normally live together in a hive, such as a hollow tree, and build a honeycomb with wax. This is a mass of six-sided cells where they store their honey and raise young bees.

Solitary bees build nests. They live alone, but often build their nests near each other. The female stores a mixture of pollen and nectar in her nest and then lays her eggs on it. When the eggs hatch, the larvae eat the stored food.

Various solitary bees make different kinds of nests. Mining bees dig tunnels in the ground. Carpenter bees may make their nests in dead branches, mason bees on rocks or in stone walls.

▽A mining bee digs out its burrow on sandy ground. Sometimes mining bees work together to dig a main tunnel, and then each female builds her own little nest in the side walls.

Wasps

As with bees, there are more species of solitary wasps than social wasps.

Solitary wasps have an unusual method for feeding their young. The female captures an insect or spider and paralyzes it with her sting. She lays an egg on its body, and the larva that hatches from the egg has a supply of fresh meat to feed on.

Most species of solitary wasp hunt a particular kind of prey, such as spiders, caterpillars, ants or bees.

△ A potter wasp drinking. Potter wasps are solitary wasps. Although adult wasps live on nectar and fruits, their larvae eat animal flesh. Potter wasps provide caterpillars for their larvae to feed on.

Social wasps include the common wasp and the hornet. They live in large colonies. Their life is similar to that of bees. There are workers and a queen. But they cannot make honey or wax, and they feed their larvae on insects.

Most species of social wasp build their nests with paper. The females produce paper by chewing up plant fibers or wood. The nests are hung from trees or shrubs or built underground in abandoned burrows.

△ A hornet with its insect prey, a large beetle. Like bees, adult wasps are vegetarians, but the social wasps feed their larvae on insects they have captured and chewed up.

▷ A wasps' nest hanging on a plant. These are paper wasps. They build open, paper nests with a single comb of cells. Other species, such as hornets, make a paper covering for their nests, with just a single entrance.

Ants and termites

Ants use their stings mainly for defense. Only a few species use them to kill or paralyze prey. Most ants use their powerful jaws to overcome prey. They sometimes also squirt acid from their rear. Some species of termites can squirt a poisonous fluid.

There are about 15,000 species of ants. In nearly all ant colonies there are three castes (classes) – queens, workers and males.

▽ A group of weaver ants combine to capture a fly. They have no stings but can overcome their prey by spraying acid from their rear end. Weaver ants are so called because of the way they stick live leaves together to make their nests. They do this by using strands of sticky thread from their larvae.

Ants are the most successful of all the insects. Some colonies have millions of members. A queen ant might live for ten to twenty years, and the workers for seven to ten.

Some species of ants are hunters, killing insects and other small animals. Others collect seeds, nectar or honeydew, a sweet liquid produced by aphids and other plant lice. Some ants raid the nests of other species, capture the young and bring them up as slaves.

△ A "soldier" termite with its nozzle-shaped head. Termites live in colonies like ants. They are plant-eaters and generally inoffensive. But a few species have special nozzle-headed soldiers which can squirt sticky fluid at enemies to disable them. Other termites defend their colonies with their large jaws.

△ The bulldog ant from Australia is probably the most dangerous ant in the world. It not only stings, but has fierce jaws that can give a painful bite. It may inject or squirt an acid into the wound caused by the bite.

◁ The black "line" on the ground is a column of army ants crossing a track in Africa. Army ants travel in colonies of tens of thousands to millions, preying chiefly on other insects.

Butterflies and moths

Many butterflies, moths and their larvae, caterpillars, have chemical defenses against their enemies. Their bright colors and markings advertise that they have an unpleasant taste or are poisonous. Predators, having tried to eat one, are unlikely to try another.

Some caterpillars have dangerous stinging hairs. Others even squirt poison.

▽ The fearsome-looking puss-moth caterpillar rears up in threatening posture. It can squirt acid at an attacker. Its main enemy is the ichneumon fly, a kind of wasp that lays eggs on it. The larvae that hatch from the eggs eat the caterpillar's body from the inside.

◁Monarch butterflies feeding on flowers. It is hard to believe that such beautiful creatures as butterflies can be poisonous. But, like many other insects, their bright colors and distinctive markings are for protection. Their warning coloration deters birds from preying on them.

Monarchs get their poison from poisonous plants that they ate as caterpillars. But some other insects make their poisons in their own bodies.

Another species, the viceroy butterfly, looks like the monarch. It is not poisonous, but predators avoid it because of its similarity to the monarch. This kind of protection is called mimicry. Other examples of mimicry include the harmless yellow and black flies that gain protection because they look like wasps.

◁ A poisonous tiger moth. The hairs on its body can sting, and the body fluids are also poisonous. Tiger moths are rarely eaten by birds, which soon learn to avoid the bold colors of these insects.

▽ The brightly colored, day-flying burnet moths are among the most poisonous of all moths. They are ignored by birds because of their foul taste.

△ The hairy caterpillar of the yellowtail moth. Its body bristles with tiny sharp spines. These inject stinging fluids that can cause severe irritation and pain if they break off in a person's skin.

▷ The brilliant colors of this West African moth warn of its poisonous nature. It has an awful taste and gives out an appalling smell.

Bugs and beetles

Bugs and beetles produce a range of poisonous fluids, mainly to put off attackers but also to kill or paralyze prey.

True bugs cannot chew. They have hollow beaks to suck blood and other juices from animals and plants. While feeding, they often pump poison into their victims.

Beetles have biting jaws. They do not inject poison, but many contain unpleasant fluids that can cause blisters if touched.

△ The ladybug is a beetle. Ladybugs help people by preying on crop-damaging insects such as aphids. Their colorful, spotted "shell" puts off predators. When disturbed, they give out a yellowish liquid, the smell and taste of which also deters attackers.

▷ The larva of a great diving beetle attacks a tadpole, grasping it with its curved jaw. Diving beetles are underwater predators. They spray out the smelly contents of digested food to put off their own enemies.

▽ An assassin bug kills a honeybee. Assassin bugs usually seize their victim with their front legs. They produce a poison in their saliva that paralyzes or kills their prey.

Other harmful insects

Some insects are harmful to people and animals without being poisonous. They might spread germs and diseases. In some parts of the world locusts devastate crops and cause famine.

Flies spread germs by landing on food. Some species of mosquito sip the blood of people and animals. Mostly this just causes an itchy irritation. But in some places mosquitoes carry serious diseases such as malaria and yellow fever.

△ A close-up of a horsefly feeding at flowers. The female also uses its stout proboscis, or beak, to pierce the skin of animals or people to suck blood. Horseflies are responsible for spreading diseases among livestock.

▷ The tsetse fly of Africa is a bloodsucking fly that transmits deadly diseases to people and livestock. It carries a tiny animal parasite that causes sleeping sickness in humans and nagana in animals.

▽ A mosquito uses its proboscis to pierce human skin and feed on blood. Mosquitoes pump in their saliva to keep the blood running freely, and this causes irritation. In the tropics and subtropics, they spread malaria-causing parasites.

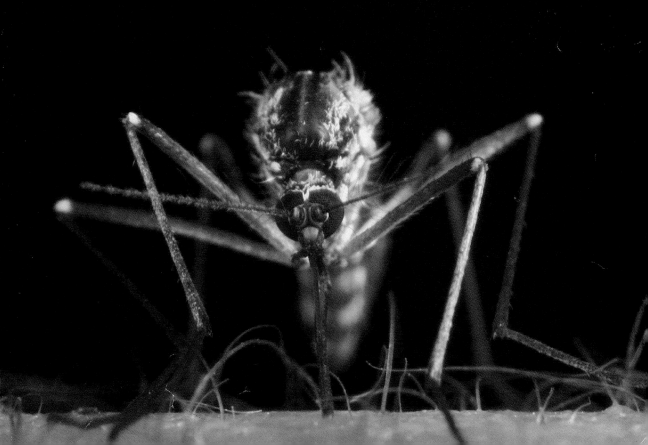

The story of poisonous insects

Poison for survival

The first insects appeared on Earth at least 400 million years ago. These six-legged creatures have been remarkably successful and have developed a wide variety of species over the years.

In the struggle for survival, poisonous species evolved (developed over millions of years). Insects are the natural food for other insects and many other animals. Those that taste unpleasant or are poisonous are less likely to be eaten. So the evolution of these features was one means of survival. The ability to sting or to inject or squirt poison also evolved as weapons of defense, or in some cases as means of capturing prey.

Life cycle of insects

Insects take different forms during the various stages of their life. A change from one form to another is called a metamorphosis. A complete metamorphosis involves four stages. These are egg, larva, pupa and adult. Most poisonous insects go through a complete metamorphosis.

Insects, like other kinds of animals without a backbone, have their skeleton on the outside. As they grow, they "molt," or cast off their skeleton, and another hardens in its place. Each molt heralds a new form or stage in the insect's life.

During the larval stage, the insect eats and grows. A caterpillar, the larval stage of a butterfly or moth, has legs because it has to search for its food. The larvae of bees and wasps do not need legs because they are surrounded by food.

Insects are inactive during the pupal stage. Their body undergoes major changes and they eventually emerge as winged adults.

△ **A monarch butterfly breaking out of its pupal case to become an adult.**

28

Harmful insects

Some insects are major pests, destroying crops or spreading disease. Nearly every cultivated plant has its own pest. Some of the worst pests are not poisonous, but they cause billions of pounds of damage to crops every year. Disease-carrying insects are not necessarily poisonous. But they are a much more serious threat to health than the stinging insects.

The bubonic plague that killed millions of people in Europe in the Middle Ages was transmitted from rats to humans by fleas. In the tropics, mosquitoes are responsible for thousands of deaths every year from malaria. Cockroaches and common houseflies transmit various diseases by soiling food.

Controlling pests

It is not easy to control insects. They are small and reproduce rapidly in large numbers. Tampering with nature can be dangerous. Insecticides, chemicals used for destroying insects, may be harmful to people. They may also upset the balance of nature by killing useful insects.

People in some areas drain swamps to destroy the breeding places of mosquitoes. Many insect pest populations are kept down by other insects, and ladybugs are brought in to control harmful insects such as aphids.

△ Beekeepers wear protective clothing to guard against stings when they tend their hives. People have been eating bees' honey for thousands of years, and began keeping bees in makeshift hives hundreds of years ago.

Useful insects

In addition to ladybugs, there are other insect predators that control harmful insect populations. Some small wasps, for example, help destroy caterpillars that damage tomato plants. Bees, wasps, butterflies, moths and some flies pollinate plants.

Facts and records

Killer ants

Army ants travel in long columns of perhaps a million or more individuals. They fan out in search of prey and eat any animal in their path. They feed mainly on other insects and spiders, but any creature that cannot burrow, climb or fly out of their way is doomed.

A single one of these ants is not dangerous, but some species of ants can give painful bites. The black bulldog ant of Australia is generally regarded as the most menacing of all ants. A sting from this fierce creature produces immediate pain and has been known to kill a person in 15 minutes.

△ Army ants combine to attack a large millipede.

Braving stings

Some animals have a natural protection from stings, and feed on wasps and bees or raid their nests and hives. Bee-eaters are birds that feed on flying insects, especially bees and wasps. The honey buzzard is a bird that breaks up wasps' nests to feed on the grubs. The African honey badger rips open bees' nests to feed on honey and larvae. Bears are also partial to honey and will often destroy hives in their search for it.

Killer bees

In their efforts to increase honey production, beekeepers have bred new varieties of honeybee. Tampering with nature, however, can sometimes backfire. In the late 1950s, a Brazilian researcher imported some bees from Africa that produced large amounts of honey. Unfortunately, they were a particularly aggressive kind. When some colonies escaped and mated with local bees, the new breed began to spread rapidly through South America.

If their hive is disturbed, these so-called killer bees will attack anything that moves. Since they arrived in Brazil, they have killed about 150 people. Countless livestock have died from their stings. By the early 1990s, they had reached some parts of Texas.

Glossary

Castes
The different kinds of insects in a colony according to the job they do – such as queens and workers.

Larva, larvae
Larvae are the nonflying young of many insects after they hatch from eggs. At the larval stage, the young look nothing like the adults. They must pass through the pupal stage before they mature.

Metamorphosis
The change from egg to adult form in insects. In a complete metamorphosis, there are two stages – larva and pupa – between egg and adult.

Mimicry
Some harmless species of insects have markings or coloration similar to that of dangerous ones. This protects them from predators, who think they are poisonous. This form of protection is called mimicry.

Molt
To shed the outer skin.

Parasite
An animal (or plant) that lives in or on another, taking food without giving anything in return. Some parasites harm or kill their hosts.

Pollinate
Flying insects pollinate flowers by taking the yellow "dust" called pollen from one flower to another. This helps the seeds to develop.

Predator
An animal that captures and eats other animals.

Pupa
The stage of development of an insect between the larval and adult stages.

Saliva
Juices formed in the mouth to start the digestion of food.

Social insects
Insects that live and work together in colonies, dependent on each other for particular jobs.

Solitary insects
Insects that live alone.

Warning coloration
Bright colors that protect poisonous insects from predators, who associate the distinctive markings with stings or an unpleasant taste.

Index